*Fish the Dead Water Hard*

Cirque Press



Published by Cirque Press

Sandra Kleven — Michael Burwell
3157 Bettles Bay Loop
Anchorage, AK 99515

Print ISBN: 978-1-68564-247-1

cirquejournal@gmail.com
www.cirquejournal.com

All artwork by David Mollet
Cover: "Smith Lake"
Pg. iv: "Forest Cascade"
Pgs. x/1: "Coal Creek"
Pgs. 12/13: "Forest Cascade"
Pgs. 40/41: "Mountains, Water and Sky"
Pgs. 58/59: "Kluane"
Pgs. 78/79: "Mountains, Water and Sky"

Book design by Emily Tallman, Poetica

# FISH THE DEAD WATER HARD

*Poems*

ERIC HEYNE

*for Alex*

## CONTENTS

### *I: The Second Shortest Day of the Year*



### *II: The Sweet Air of Terra*

## *III: Habanerror*



## *IV: A Sucker for Low Tides*

# *I: The Second Shortest Day of the Year*

## *Accretions*

A stiff white world built
by two months' growth
of hoarfrost without wind
chimes a new color each hour
as the sun sneaks up
from the south. But one
day of chinook and
it's all gone to black and white,
the spruce shedding water
and swallowing light. Seems
the winter's burden dissolved
in the south wind's shade
before I knew how hard
I wanted to stay froze.

# *Found*

*Fetters of a burning chain*
*~ Julia Ward Howe*

Stained white bark grows around links rusted
to the colors of earth, one fat hook wedged
into place, the other end buried in leaves, clenched
to the ground by willow and horsetail roots.
Something was anchored once to this tree,
hauling itself from the mud it was stuck in,
or else the tree itself was marked and bound
for falling. Whichever it was, the arms
that looped the logging chain around this birch
forgot it, like Frost's well-made woodpile
abandoned to rot, far from the fire
it was meant to feed. Ochre flakes of dust
on my hands smell like caves and old ice, links
to a dug-up grave waiting refilling.

## *Inukshuk*

A stone unman stands
alone on the tundra, blind,
planed face giving nothing
away. Vole-gnawed antlers
bleach in the dim sun. Sharp
discs of snow tumble
westward under the clear sky.
A few flakes melt in the fount
of a speckled ptarmigan
shell. The hieroglyphic lichen
spell out their slow story, black
and orange, in a dead language.
The dull muttering of guns
rumbles downwind, and someone,
awaiting migration, finds
this stack of stones on the horizon
and is no longer alone.

## *Sign*

In the broad upper valley of Kuyuktuvuk Creek
where now-defunct glaciers shouldered
downslope, shoving the mountains apart,
a brown bear lopes over the pass right at us,
then disappears in a shallow swale.
A mile down the valley we stop to catch
our breath and watch a fat arctic ground
squirrel watch us from under the lip
of an ice shelf. Then there's that bear again,
not behind us but alongside up the curve
of the valley. Hauling ass up the opposite
side we stumble across a Dall sheep skull
laid out equilaterally from its two thick horns.

Mounted in a mossy patch green against gray rock
of the Kuyuktuvuk streamcourse lies the rusted
skeleton of a Winchester, stock rotted away.
Who laid down his rifle in the middle of the Brooks Range?

On the way up that morning we regretted not
pitching our tent in a patch of flat clean sand just
a hundred yards on from where we'd collapsed,
and now there are fresh ten-inch grizzly tracks.

## *Inversion*

It's warm up here, fifteen below.
Chickadees sweep towards me
from the tops of birch trees
then veer off, seeing something
in the plate glass not quite air.
Their bustle brushes snow from
branches like explosions backlit
by the orange sun still midway
through its hour-long rise.
The cold of thirty thousand feet
has dropped like sediment from
ocean air onto the valley floor,
the ice fog fossilizing all trace
of life. Aging aspen stretch
their skinny trunks like kelp and I
am anchored in this houseboat waiting
for the tide of winter to turn.

## *Sluggishness*

The slow wing beats
Of an out of season eagle
Against the thick air

The front-step ice that
Takes its evaporative time
Pulling on winter's frozen tail

The gloom of noon
Filtered by a life sentence
Of holiday listlessness

The moose-chewed willows
That well into April still
Refuse to spit out catkins

The spawned-out start-of-school
Salmon shedding flesh, losing
Ground to the low current

Silent meals and the muffled
Clatter of dishes when the one
Whose turn it is gets around to it

## *Aviglyphs*

For a few days they're so loud you don't hear them
anymore, but walking between two dorms the echo
makes you look up at just the right moment. And

there they go, passing over at three depths, in three
vectors: a squall of ducks, above them a V of geese,
and deep at the bottom of the sky a check mark

of cranes, all honking in their own dialects, but writing
one language on the sky, and you feel lucky and dizzy
parsing the migratory air, this cuneiform revelation.

## *Minus*

On the second-shortest day of the year
The bottom has fallen out of the sky
As if the end were somewhere near

And we have nowhere to be but here.
There's nothing unspoken between you and I
On the second-shortest day of the year

Except one or two of our deepest fears—
But we'll find a way to keep up those lies.
And if the end is somewhere near

Why would we anything but oblige
The urge to let sleeping dogs die?
I feel the end is somewhat near
On the second-shortest day of the year.

# *II. The Sweet Air of Terra*

## *Valentine's Day 1999*

On the first day of your first cold snap—
polar air plopping its fat bottom
smack in your warm lap, ice fog wrapping
its clammy arms around you so tightly
you gasp, and your tears freeze—
you look over at me with that
petulant face I just can't resist,
as if all this weather were my fault.

One drain freezes up. The steering is thick.
The sun has gone missing. A sheath of ice
sprouts from a vent on the roof outside
my office, like a limestone chrysalis.
Fractal knives feather the windows with
frost carvings, and the dry air squeezes
out snow crystals like the patient
residue of a distant dust storm.

Walking in this is like seeing the earth
from space, a painting in an endless frame.
Who knew we were so alone? No one
wants to go out, even to buy food.
A kind of peace comes over us all, as we
let go of those things it turns out we don't need.
There's nothing to do but pool our heat, and
find reasons to stay home, in bed, in arm's reach.

*Name Day*

Late in the white night I'm lying in wait
for rabbits, plotting BB-gun murder
of flower-munching pests. Today we chose
your name, after we watched silent sound waves
carve you out in cross-section and give up
your sex. Mom catches up on this week's debt
of insomnia. No bunnies yet.
The late-July rains have hesitated.
The sun must be down—there are no shadows.
A freight train, oil tanker cars bound south,
whistles for the Sheep Creek crossing, and I
smile to think of you growing up hearing
those trains. You'll be eight or nine for the next
peak in the snowshoe hare cycle—
will you ask me not to shoot them, or take
aim yourself, grave with the chore of saving
your parents' garden from those predators.
Who's to say? Not I, not tonight. For now
you're busy dreaming whatever dreams come
before birth, protected from your father's
best intentions, safe on your dark homestead.

## *Diagnose This*

*This is the recipe for the pie I would have made*
*~ Sue Hubbell*

So on the day Hunter tells me they'll have to do a biopsy
I'm trying to find distractions,
But keep running up against grim reminders.
A journal arrives with a piece by me in it,
And while I try not to think of it as
The Last Thing I Will Ever Publish,
The article next to mine is about the emerging genre
Of terminal illness autobiographies.
Great. Enough of that.
So I pick up my text to prepare for class
And the first thing I need to read is "Thanatopsis,"
That wise old poem by a very young William Cullen Bryant
Advising me to "approach [my] grave,
Like one who wraps the drapery of his couch
About him, and lies down to pleasant dreams."
We'll see about those pleasant dreams.
Meanwhile the email has a reminder about
This year's Dead Writers fundraiser, and I hear
Graduate students trying to remember
Who has died recently and might make good fodder.
"Next you'll be telling me Dr. Seuss is dead,"
One says, and I can't be sure of the irony.
I do not want it in the lungs
I do not want it in my tongue
I don't want cancer of the gall
I do not want it, not at all.
Now things are really out of control
And I wonder if this time next year
Someone will be reading this poem,
And what a damn shame it would be
If that someone wasn't me.

## *Cottonwood Dreams*

welcome shade every June on the sandy bottoms
        of the Pandhandle, New Mexico, eastern Colorado
                as my family fled Dallas like vanned pioneers

summer seeds clogging screen windows, clotting
        on clothes, piling up in corners, blown by the
                west wind like a freak snowstorm or mutant orgasm

". . . the dead cottonwood is troubling in being
        so appropriate and so inappropriate a repository
                for the bones of the cannibalized chiefs . . ."

that tall grove growing out of gravel at the head
        of Hart Lake, the first and best campsite, en route
                to the crest trail that went north and south forever

thirty years of this tree, of staring up
        at the slowly brightening sky through a grid
                of leaves, and I'm still dreaming, still scrunched

down in my old cotton sleeping bag
        shrinking from the cold, not ready to move on,
                not yet willing to wake up

The quoted lines in stanza three are taken from page 77 of Karl Kroeber's *Retelling/ Rereading: The Fate of Storytelling in Modern Times.*

## *Stepmother*

*I recline by the sills of the exquisite flexible doors*
*- Walt Whitman*

You were half my age now when we showed up
in your college-town two-bedroom daylight-
basement apartment, three kids invading
your honeymoon. Packing for a week we'd left
all our toys, and in the careless spite of a custody
battle never saw them again. You helped us build
cigar-box-and-rubber-band guitars, and we sang
along to "Yesterday" and "Little Deuce Coupe."

The best thing was how from the first you talked
to us like we were worth listening to, a skill
you'd learned at Bank Street School. You never
yelled or spanked, though your husband did,
and for this high-strung perfectionist eldest
afraid of love moving out (like his parents took
turns doing for years) that was deep respite,
a quiet room and all the time I wanted just to read.

Once on our weekly drive to the nearest Dallas
Public Library branch (too far to bike) I complained
that soon there would be no science fiction left
unread. When you laughed and walked me over
to the long shelves of strange grown-up books, it felt
like my lander had opened to the sweet air of Terra.

Now our daughter, raised in a house full of your
paintings, will have her own chance to learn from
your love of doors, demolitions, scaffolds, all
the possibilities of a wall, the way any ugly unbuilt
place can be shaped into its mysterious self by one
who takes what she's given and makes it hers.

## *Genus Nymphalis*

"Don't step on it!" my daughter warned
as we lugged in the grocery bags
from the garage. It looked like a leaf,
orange and brown, ragged-edge wings.
She brought it in for her "collection,"
until it moved, morphed into a pet.
Ignorant of the secret life of butterflies,
I had no idea they survived the cold
in Fairbanks; this winter-wakened
Compton Tortoiseshell (we googled it)
was as big a surprise as a yeti would have been.
It lapped up orange juice from my daughter's
hand, flew around her room and returned
to that outstretched palm, emerging by day
and going back into the butterfly house
by night. A domesticated insect!
Even knowing the end was near did not
prevent the tears a few days later—not hers
but mine, ashamed to weep for a bug.

## *Home Visit*

In a south Texas small-town nursing home,
the last that would have her, my mother
dies as she lived, alone, at her own pace.
The August heat is too much for her room's
air-conditioning, fills my rental car
like a balloon, and finally brings the storm.
Accordion music wails down the hall.
A skinny, cheerful, bearded patriarch
with tall sons and skirted daughters roams
the hallways leaving tracts and taping up
crayon drawings by the youngest, captioned
"Jesus loves you." Out the window past her
birdfeeder hard rain falls on the highway.
She says she wants to die, but doesn't want
it to hurt. More accordion music.
The rain lets up. Residents roll by down
the hall, some swinging their arms together
like wheelchair racers, some alternating
in the old way of walking, one or two
shuffling crossed feet in a quick dance step.
Accordion music, with piano accompaniment.
The oxygen cart wheezes and bubbles.
She looks like her own mother, but older.
Her lead-gray hair is in the same pixie
cut she wore forty years ago, a young
faculty wife serving martinis at
parties that stretched long past the cocktail hour.
The rain picks up again, slowing the traffic,
slapping the ground like thumbs beating time.
She sips near-beer. I eat another chocolate-
sealed donut from the machine. Across the hall
a woman falls getting into bed, and while

we wait for the mandated ambulance
she asks me to turn on the weather channel.
I'm hypnotized by the repeated pulse
of Doppler bloom, wind and rain mutated
into color. When it lets up there's still
no ambulance. I say goodbye, weave my
way down the crowded hall for the last time,
drive off down the state road, crossing swollen
creeks fed by sodden fields, passing giant
American flags marking each new housing
development, the city laying claim
to land it had left alone for a while.

## *Stargazer*

Belly swelling slightly under crossed arms,
left over right, nose rising like the prow
of a stone ship steering by the stars on
a night passage among the Cyclades,
her knees are just bent, her feet *en pointe*:
a pose without repose, neither standing
nor lying, not of this world. Here, we lock
our knees, spread our legs, and lower our heads
against the sharp wind blowing off the north
of Naxos, clawing at our clothes and hair
as if to strip us naked, bald as stone
for our return trip across the dark sea.

## *From Hellas*

I.
Our first day and night in Paros
the wind blew relentless, cold,
straight out of the north over the Aegean.
When we bobbed up out of the warm ocean
our heads ached until we ducked again.
The house we'd borrowed was built low
facing south, honoring that north wind.
This morning only a small breeze slips
across from Naxos. Chugs and whines
of fishing boats carry along
the water and up the rocks to the house.
A kestrel (or what they have here like them)
hunts the prickly scrub between low stone walls.
Tiny black and white birds bob in and out
of the juniper. The garden still blooms this late
in autumn. Back home it's snowing already.
The lights of Lefkis formed a triangle
on the mountain slopes last night,
perfectly framed in the window as we lay
under a white comforter and marveled
at our luck, until the wind died
and mosquitoes helped us feel at home.

II.
At the same time every day the accordion
player passes through the street below
our classroom. *Why here?* we ask. *Do people*
*throw him coins?* His repertoire is so clichéd
even we Americans know one or two.
How does he live? How do any of them?

III.
Over breakfast at a beach café in Aegina
we watch a middle-aged bikinied woman
beat an octopus against the stone seawall.
The waiter, the waitress, the boss at the till—
waiting for us, or someone just like us—
remind me of the man who hung back
at the dock, reserving his excellent English,
and only when we looked lost asked
politely if we needed a place to stay.
Hoi-polloi, proletariat, demos, lives
dependent on other lives, on coins
dropping from some balcony above.

IV.
Dear guests, we go now, this way.
Dear guests, again I tell you
all the yellow part, everywhere
you see yellow, that is gold.
Dear guests, again I tell you
the floor is not painted, all this
is different woods. Do you have
questions? No? Okay, we go.

V.
We ate a hurried prix fixe lunch in Asia
after crossing the bridge in a pouring rain
just to say that we'd been on another continent.
Later the rain abated and we took a boat
up the Bosphorus to read the water
that has always been the theme of this story.

VI.
Somewhere in the haze down there,
across the gulf, is Kirra, where cruise ships
dock to run their tourists up to Delphi.
It's crazy warm for November, days
too short for such heat. Back in Athens

the Plaka cafes are shadowed
by the Acropolis in mid-afternoon.
Here time has absconded. Roads
wind patient and empty into the haze,
grapes go unharvested, raki undrunk,
the narrow distances of Greece elongated
like its history, and here at the navel
of the world we're still asleep and dreaming,
waiting for the prophecy we've paid for.

## *Autumn on the Aegean*

*We don't know we're all sailors out of work…*
*– George Seferis*

One thing Greece still does well is ferries.
Aboard the Knossos Palace on the night
crossing from Crete I ponder the arche-
ologically incoherent icon
of Minoan Lines looming above us:
the Lily Prince pieced together from three
different frescoes, two men's arms, a woman's
headdress. Over the last few days I'd flashed
my teacher I.D. card to get in free
at Knossos, Phaistos, Gortyna, Malia,
all the museums, feeling rich as Croesus
and grateful to the whole Greek nation.
In Hania they gave us a shopping day
and one student bought an anthology
of five Greek poets. Using traveling
light as my excuse for cheapness, I borrowed
her copy. Seferis was the one who
swept me up, and the poems that put me back
in his world all invoked ships and the sea.
Every time we make the slow zig-zag out
of Piraeus I stand at the railing
staring—not back at the Acropolis
but out at all the other ships: the fleet
of freighters scattered in the Gulf,
fantasy yachts, fishing boats, tugs, long strings
of tiny racing sails, and most of all
the ferries, fast on their hydrofoil feet
or towering like buildings on water.
Back in Athens we're told that tomorrow,
the Seventeenth of November, would be
a good day for Americans to stay

home, read poetry, and maybe think back
over the four millennia and more
these shores have been stricken by trade and war.

## *The Archaeologist*

He is a servant of the gods, a humble
priest in the church of scientific inquiry.
There is almost no flesh on him; what he eats
is somewhere between ambrosia
and human food. He will take a drink
if the time and place are propitious.
He is surrounded by nymphs and minor
heroes—that is, girls who have an inkling
of their power and boys without a clue.
In a house by the sea in the southeast
fringes of Athens he lives with his family:
a mother losing her children daily,
a sister keeping house for all, her husband
come down from the peaks of Tibet
to the plains and worn-down mountains of Attica.
Within this *oikos* they speak mostly Swedish,
though he has Greek and English and German
and others when they're called for.
Wearing his fanny pack like a monk's cincture,
he crosses his arms and tilts his head
patiently, waiting for some kind of light
to creep in behind your eyeballs and say
*Eureka!* He keeps his beard near the theoretical
limits of trimmed, and when he smiles
and pulls the grey mop of his bangs
back from his eyes like a black-and-white movie
Bedouin removing a turbaned scarf after
a dusty ride, you know you had best sit tight,
for it will be worth the silence soon enough.

## *Gijón*

Beyond the beach full of delirious dogs
a sharp blue sea sweeps in on
steep winter waves.
Women in furs and their daughters in short skirts
promenade along the seawall, laughing
at the dogs' antics.
The tide is well out but turning.
The sea will go to green, the hills gray,
the sky squeezed thin between,
in the storm that can just be seen offshore.
Littered around this town of fishermen
and coal miners we stepped over
red handbills proclaiming a general strike.
There was no date on them. They might
have been here since the Romans
abandoned this seaport outpost
to the bureaucrats of a later imperium.

## *A Story of Seduction*

I. Sometimes it seems

this is the way it's supposed to be:
the clean, colorful city rising up
the long ridge, with hills becoming
mountains on two sides, the ocean
just out of sight to the north, shut-up
factories and the mines in the valleys
along the rail lines, sheep and goats
grazing smack against the edge
of the city, the compact old part
with its maze of tight, angled streets
and all the streets changing names
every couple of blocks, the people
different in subtle ways but so friendly,
mild weather but assertive seasons,
trains in every direction, a fine bus
system for when you don't feel like walking,
and over it all some kind of filter,
a sea-haze, a dream, a looming deadline,
and the passing days marked only by books
read and shelved and by rows of empty bottles
of good cheap wine waiting to be carted
out to the appropriate receptacle.

II. From outside looking in

the cities of Spain are still walled,
towering apartment buildings
each with its first floor of restaurants
and kiosks and highly specialized
businesses. The real life is inward,
looking down on tiny playgrounds

and mini-plazas, from metal-sheathed
windows that only the owners ever
appear at. They host each other outdoors,
at a bodega or cafe, never
in their own homes. This trig little city
will hold out against the barbarians,
and leave me circling like the traffic on
the ronda, clinging to an inner lane,
not ready to chance any spoke of the wheel.

## *El Colegio Inglés de Asturias*

Every morning she boards the crowded bus to ride
out of Oviedo to her posh British school,
Jolly Olde England in the Spanish countryside.
At recess the air billows with high-pitched Spanish
but she knows only the English they speak in class.
North Sea weather rings down the limestone coast its brisk
changes, sparkling blue to dismal gray in moments,
bare arms in the sun, furs on in the wind. The cost
of our sabbatical here is paid in the coin
of the middle-school realm, by turns boring and cruel,
the junta of mean girls having ostracized her
and the busy teachers handing out busywork.
There is only one lesson to learn. Watching her
move down the row of bus seats, I wish I could take
some of this pain for her. But that's not how it works.
This kid will always have to eat my just desserts.

## *New Season – for Heath*

*Whether thou get'st them green, or lets them seed*
*- Edward Taylor*

First frost of the year came that morning with
a frenzy of feeding in the chokecherry
as thrush fattened up for the long flight south.
First day of classes. Can it be forty years
since I was a freshman? How can I have
any notion what these kids are feeling?

My father, who drove me west two thousand
miles to college, a rental-car version
of our cross-country trips by micro-bus
every summer, is dead now fourteen years.
My stepmom, along then for the ride, turned
seventy-five this week, must have given
up her birthday for my delivery
that Labor Day.
                    This year it was Sam's turn
to start college, until she was summoned
home for her cousin's funeral.
                                        I try
to understand what they're feeling,
my brother and sister-in-law, my niece,
the new world they've awakened to.
Annabel and I take the red-eye south
to a city I've never seen, a house
not quite lived in that they will abandon
to grief as if it were contaminate.

The service has no hint of the beliefs
we grew up so embedded in; without
those rituals we must reinvent our mourning,
sharing a flash of Heath in a cousin's
eye, recalling patches of his humor,

casting his death against our childrens' lives
like a harsh light pinning them in stiffened
poses.
            Now we will scatter again, north
and west, back to our separate rites and lives,
the angel of death having made her choice
and passed on, leaving us in fall to mourn
the impossible lives of the living.

## *Bitter April Suite*

I.

The chickadees are singing, they ache
to be nesting, they've waited out the long
subarctic winter scrapping with redpolls
for seeds from the forest of domestic
feeders while other birds (wimps!) winged it
on south to warmer weather, and now
they're first on the ground, raring to make
avian whoopee.

But it's a wicked cold spring we're having,
twenty below last night and the snow
still deep, sarcastically white when it
ought to be dirty and on the way out.
I'm just as pissy as the birds, sick
of shoveling snow across upthrust ruts
left by the paper guy's truck and the slick
stretch where the water man spills his gallon
or two every time he delivers, sick
of pushing piles farther out over
the edge and sinking thigh deep in misstep.

There's plenty of light, all our photo-
sensitive hormones are triggering,
clothes coming off despite the cold, and it
will be spring, dammit, if we have to sing
and drink and stay up late until it comes,
as it always does come, uncaring,
more loved than loving, a seasonal slut
that will have us tearing our fur out.

II.

Drifts pile up despite the clear blue sky; old
snow blows off roofs and into odd corners,

this April snow—not *fall*, more *fling*—
all the showers we get just yet as temps
huddle below the freezing mark. Liquid
sheens leak across southern exposures
and pool in sun-snagging angles. This too,
too solid flesh of earth just will not melt
into any semblance of spring, and we
have more light than we can use and less
heat than we deserve.

III.
Smack at the end of this long cold
month, as I said to myself for the umpteenth morning
*At least this is the last time I'll have to*
*shovel snow this year*, it hit me: I'd missed
the anniversary of my father's death.

Maybe it's a relief: thirteen years now
since we four stood looking down on a man
we'd always looked up to and heard him breathe
his last breath. Then
jumped
out of our skins
when there turned out to be one more. Not like
he was fighting it—he wanted to get
this thing over with, stop being a bother.
More like taking his time with that last step.
When he had no more inspiration it
was time to expire.

The frozen heart of winter still beats
this April long after it should have died
and made way for spring. Though summer crowds
the wings, lights up, ready for its entrance,
something has missed its cue, foetal mud
still sleeping, the river frozen quiet,
pale aspen branches creaking and empty.

## *Post*

After we make love, once we disengage
and sprawl, after you dig up your p.j.'s
where they were kicked off and trampled way down,
after the good-night kiss that always stays
our lips a moment softer on such nights,
I flip around and find a swelling moon
athwart some invisible mountains, bright
enough (just) to decode the dark. That spruce
frozen tight in one trapezoidal pane
lingers like a screenshot while stars stray on.
I've forgotten other views, other frames.
What would I give for this not to be gone?
But I'm already dreaming by the time
the boiler winds the clock of ticking pipes.

## *III. Habanerror*

## *Death and the Earth's Weather*

Pelt mottled gray and white, April's
snowshoe hare is exposed both on
and off the melting snow.
                                        Castaneda's
and Casanova's sly creations—
those two Don Juans, the shaman
and the ladies' man—took their cues
from death, the big one and
the little: One must have both
a powerful will and a stiff world
on which to impose it.

We love to conflate climate
and weather, like the global
warming that made it rain last November.
But green-up wasn't late
this year after all,
just right
on
schedule. Heat waves back at you.

This is the same train we rode as children
up in the dome car, folding our beds down
in the sleeper on our wedding night,
listening for the crossing whistle
up late with the baby. Same train,
same snowshoe hares, same death
in the stern wake of a wavering jet stream.

## *Sonnet for Solace*

Just assume you're still in love
even while standing at the door
talking back across your shoulder
with one foot over the threshold.
Love is not a building you're in,
not over your head like deep water,
nor a wave pattern like REM sleep,
not like being in Dutch or like Flint.

But some time after all this time
it's hard to separate love from a house
you've kept clean and filled up with
stuff, like the new good shaman mask

that might protect us
if we had anything to fear.

## *A Lover's Request*

Hurry up and love me before I can't
do it anymore. It's coming, I can tell.
All my senses are going—weak eyes,
tinnitus, proprioception failures
measured by bruises from random
solid body encounters, and I can't say
for sure about taste and smell but
nothing savors like it used to.
Hurry up and love me before you won't
get what you deserve. Hurry up so
we can take it slow, lollygag naked,
no pressure except the pressures we
choose to exert, tongue and finger,
pubic bone and clitoris and lips.
Hurry up and kiss me before
this moon thins out completely,
before the chores need doing again,
before I forget all I've learned
about you and me and our anatomy
and I forgo more flexibility. Hurry

## *Not Ever*

How it feels to be gravid
I'll never know. What else can't
I be? As tall as my father,
young again, at peace
with scorpions, quiet of voice
or quiet of mind, unjudg-
mental, unorphaned,
skilled at any musical instrument,
alive in a hundred years,
one of the faithful,
the world's greatest lover,
a man, a man, a man
at home in the world.

## *Tourist Dreams*

My lately dreams are all vacations at last
resorts. In the remaining box of Girl Scout
Thin Mints one is backwards in its stack
like a secret message from the factory:
10,000 marbles and one Snicker-Snack.
Pools, lakes, hotels, mountain trails, guides
and waiters serving up the stories of my mind,
places I've almost been to many times long
ago or maybe it was just the past yar?
The only winter left is buried in
municipal dump-humps of black rock
so you'd never know it was snow
beneath. Tomorrow we'll dream
of strange life escaping like red algae
sunning and cutting albedo on the back
of a melting glacier, shedding centuries
away, away, on the road to Mandalay.

## *Grouse Encounter*

Head-down out the door in the morning I'm
spooked by the explosion of a ruffed grouse
taking flight in my face, interrupting
the walking dream I was still indulging,
and once my heart starts up again it goes
faster to make up for missing that beat.
Just out of reach in a birch the fat cock
sticks out his chest, raises his hackles, struts
upright, tells those hens he ain't scared of me
even though I snuck up on him like that.

## *Notes from Above Ground*

Fetching the paper this morning
 I walked down the drive in the bright
  glare of a waning three-quarter moon,
its edges pulsing in the last few flakes
 of snow. A gray owl's woo-hoo
  froze me, and I waited to hear it again,
then something made me look back over
 my shoulder. The shadow
  of a skinny black spruce stretched
fifty feet straight at me like the blade
 of a huge moondial, like the cold's
  own claw singling me out for favor.
I shivered, and waited, but the owl
 had nothing more to say. Unbelieving,
  I still wished for a charm to ward off
The close attentions of my unknown enemy.

## *High Water*

It's August and getting dark again,
but we can still see the ball coming
at 10:00. I'm pooped and sandy,
three beers in, about to go home,
but someone's yelling at us
from two blocks away, waving
his arms, and I take off toward him
as fast as my flip-flops will carry me.

Lying flat on the street he puffed out
his story: the outboard died, the current
shoved his riverboat under sweepers
on the near shore and it flipped.
The older girls jumped, but mom
and the baby are still under the hull,
go, go, that way, you'll see it
pinned against the bank upside down.

I hoisted the gunwale while Brad
dove in and brought them out. We hauled
her sodden up the slippery bank then
passed him, heavy as a sandbag, up.
Brad blew into their blue lips til the EMTs
showed up. Barefoot on the dark rocks
we figured out that neither made it,
and our part in their story was over.

## *YOLO Solo*

*Live in the moment*
they say, and say,
and say. But
where else can
one go live except
this cell block,
a present from
God before the real
comeuppance, time's
arrow all ways
shooting through your
bullsheart, *alas*
this cubicle we
vacate every chance
we get, dipping back
to that sweet past or
hinting forward
to a funner future,
to generate some
dream momentum?

## *Dislocation Is My Home*

being ready to go

being on the verge
                    of retiring

letting someone else have that office
          run that program,
                    make those same mistakes

hugging the pillow, drooling

strangely calm about going
          despite showing few signs
                    of decrepitude but orneriness

But what about missing out on
                    what happens next

or leaving things in such a mess?

Isn't there more to be doing more
                    needing to be done?

Yes, by someone, else

at lasting there's no sequel, it's
          end of the series, volume X-Z,
                    seventh game, final extra turn

being ready to go early or late

being on the edge of something, dreaming of going

loving the past too much and all of
                    you less than your desserts

being just precisely almost that son of a bitch

## *Inhumanity*

ravens call in wolves to break
the hide of moose and caribou
carcasses, and all are fed

my gut's not a mere colony of bacteria
but a metropole, a teeming city
of uncooperative aliens coinciding

lately this house feels like
a newbie's ten-gallon tank
of short-time incompatible fish

I wish I could fondle the steel-
plastic-ceramic sculpture
they grew in there on my hips

at seven you loved to scoop up dragonfly
larvae, tadpoles, boatmen, beetles
from the tiny pond at the bottom of our road

dreams of the many-in-one,
love and cohabitation, none of us
just the thing we thought we were

## *Not-hunting*

A rotted birch drapes across the autumn
ground like a Dali watch. The still-white bark
is supple, hardwood gone so soft it's tough
to picture this tree as ever straight or tall.
The sootblack aluminum bones of a dead
camp chair frame a rectangle of dead moss:
still-life without wildlife, spoor of a long-
gone hunter not patient enough to truck
out this trash he packed in so hopefully.
We've seen no moose all afternoon.
I came along for the walk, and to help
haul out the meat if we got lucky with this
special permit hunt in the Goldstream flats.
The strange warm fall drags on. The road
remains slippery, the mud almost deep enough
to turn us around, long after it ought
to have frozen solid, and there's no snow
and no smell of snow in the air, just a rainbow
cresting off the swell of the low sun and one
or two drops of rain. Dry enough for good
walking, though, with the yellow leaves
splotched and faded but still hanging on.
Besides lugging the gun, my buddy (the man
with the special cow permit) stops now and then
to stroke the willow branches with his imitation
antler and grunt off toward the distant hills.
I desperately wanted to see a moose fooled
by a sawed-off orange juice bottle.
We saw tracks aplenty and gnawed willows,
but no big bodies, no meat for our freezers,
just a raven or two rooting for us,
an ancient spruce bigger than I knew they grew
around here, the fanciest hunting stand west
of the Mississippi, and that supple birch curved
along the forest floor like a reclining nude.

## *Pityfest*

I much prefer soft tissue work.
Least of all I like the neck snap.

Last night my daughter carved our jack-
o-lantern to the moth-mouthed Clarice
Starling from *Silence of the Lambs*,
and just the day before we watched
Macbeth's head raised, a bloody crown,
like the headless horseman aiming
his pumpkin at poor Ichabod.

How long before I'll need adjustment?
Before I'll be rubbed out again?

There's just a wisp of cloud to warm us.
A half moon waxes, leftover
snow cowers in northern shadows
with rain in the forecast tomorrow
(and tomorrow). We put a face
on fall and hope the moose don't munch
it up until at least All Souls.

The bare birch have a beauty that
the needled trees never get to feel.

Today the creaking of my knees
sounds like ravens, the strangled croak
they make when they don't deign to talk
but can't shut up. Each year's decline
toward solstice Macbeth's bitterness
comes closer. I root for the moose,
the lambs, poor Ichabod, and me.

## *IV. A Sucker for Low Tides*

## *Ghost Ship*

From fifty feet up on petrified waves
of rusty rock windrows the ditch runs due
west, a bright strip of still water. Below,
the dredge floats like a skeletal steamboat
moored to the ice skim on its shadowed port.
Rot moves slow so far north, and tailing rock
this size is almost sterile. Giants hosed
the soil from these hills and stacked their bones
in open-air crypts. On either side fall's
birches' turmeric leaves are backlit, spruce
broken between them like shafts of darkness.
Bald-faced hornets crawl along the ground, too
weak to reach their nests in corrugated
nooks where hibernating queens dream alone.

## *In Green Alaska*

That particular silver light slanting
off the aspen leaves, evoking olive
groves rinsed in Iberian sunlight and
spread out to dry against the windy frame
of plowed red fields, utterly out of place
in the subarctic, is left in the wake
of leaf miners scraping meals from the green
of whole groves and hills, weakening the trees
over years, sapping deeply stored sugars.
Farther south the beetle-killed spruce are red
across the slopes; as it warms they'll move north.
My daughter may live to see the new trees
move in, leaf, needle, and bole, remaking
the light and the shape of the sky at dusk.

## *Listening to John Haines Read His Poetry*

Well past seventy now, he still speaks
with that deep resonance like the voice
of God, perfect for such fine oracular poems.
They seem to echo up from a well
in the earth, or descend straight from heaven,
the original logos, that very same word
that boomed out in the beginning.
He stands there at the podium,
out of place, a survivor like those
Norwegian bachelor trappers
he wrote about, relic of a time before
highways or fast food outlets, a colder
and quieter time, with fewer voices.
He ends each poem with a quiet "hmm,"
maybe of surprise, or satisfaction,
as if he had forgotten us, or the poems.
Most were early, from the homesteading days,
*Winter News*, the book that got him heard
back East when poetry was serious stuff.
Now that too seems like a different age.
Today we have slams and Nike ads,
creative writing programs and journals
by the score, among which John ekes out
a life of academic subsistence,
depositing him here tonight. Come
Judgement Day, when all is buried in
a final rain of frequencies, I'll be left
with the echo of a deep voice reading
short poems from a place we dimly remember.

## *Candle Ice*

Candle ice slips in sheets off the shelf
over the river where it sneaks out into Lower
Tangle. Small grayling gang the shallows
for what floats by, old lake trout hover
in deeper water for stray unwary grayling,
and our waders double as overgrown
breakup boots making us fluent in all terrains
and dangerous to the fish (we think).
So many things to be discovered then:
the fit of our bodies against the tent floor contours,
what it meant to love without competing,
the few roads and many long roadless views
we could cover and yet never run out of
(we thought). The best time to fish this spot,
with jigs bouncing like waterlogged grubs
from fast water to still, is just when the seasons
are flipping over, first open water like this
and the first freezing days just a few months away.

## *This Old World*

The apocalypse is going to need some
really old words. Will *wagon* serve our needs,
or will it be *wain*? Will *pigs* be Biblical
enough, or *swine*? Darkness waits at both ends
of this tunnel. A waxing three-quarter
moon hovers over the frozen hills just
before dusk, but I can't bear to watch it
go down. Something is squeezing the life out
of us, pricking our thumbs, the child's balloon
of this world flinging its diminished skin
across the nursery of space and time.

## *Ed*

Sarah came to fetch me from the arctic
entry of the soup kitchen, and the door
swung shut behind her. Locked out
while our Celebration of Writing chili
darkened in the hot oven, she paced,
I tut-tutted, we texted for help and shared
that sense of failure when defeated
by simple things like locks and carelessness.

But then he showed up, the man
who ran the soup kitchen and all
its network of support, let us in, saran-
wrapped the chili for us, talked us down,
warmed us up with his calm
competence, just days before he took
his own life. What door locked
behind him on a frigid day?

## *Scavengers and Predators*

Spading a weeded-in bed brought
little ants swarming
from the corner of the creosoted sleepers.
I sprayed them out.
They flowed like six-legged lava down the path
to the orchard
and set up shop in the middle of things.
I sprayed them out.
Decamping more deviously this time, they
dug in among
the daises and lupine in an unmowed strip
where they live still.

Big carpenter ants filed out from their
nest in dead birch
along the superhighway of gutter hose
(and beneath it)
up into my daughter's room, where the drones
flew out in droves.
I sprayed and sprayed, but they came back.
We called in pro-
fessionals, got a tutorial, traced the back
entrance through grass,
and got a re-spray (on the house)
when they came back.

When the crabapples are thick with pink
blooms and shimmer
with swallowtails and bumblebee moths,
sometimes we'll see
a butterfly drop from mid-air as if fainting,
taken down by
the sting of a hunting bald-faced hornet
and hauled off to

paper nests camouflaged in the aspens.
They'll also prey
on our salmon steaks and barbecued ribs
in a dry year.

Last year was dry and warm, everything sticky
with aphid shit,
rose leaves curled and sere, too late for the bag
of ladybugs
we should have liberated weeks earlier.
Some stick around
a whole season and next summer copulate
in twos and threes
on the railings, leaving orange jello eggs
that hatch fat ant-
like wingless larvae looking nothing like
the voracious
aphid eaters they will grow up to be.

## *Waiting for the Revolution*

Spring haze obscures the mountains, middle
distance making your acquaintance
in the interim (until the heavy air of fall
brings the far peaks up close again).
You wouldn't think, to look at all that snow,
that it was spring. Shows what you know.
Easter makes a funny fertility festival here,
when the birch and aspen have only begun
thinking about their greenish duties,
and those garish long-leaved ads for spring—
tulip, crocus, iris, daffodil—
are just a gleam in the antsy gardener's eye.
Only the pussy willows dare to push
this envelope, and only where they have survived
the browse of that annoying moose and her calf
whose snacking smacked the dogwood branches
against our bedroom window in the wee hours.
Chasing them off does no good. They just come back,
like winter, soon enough.

## *Nowcasting*

*Fish the dead water hard*
the guide called out as we
drifted by. Easy for him to say.
He must know this river way too well,
floating it all summer long
mostly in the heavy Yakutat rain
rather than these rare blue skies.
I'm agog at his skill with the oars,
how he bobs and weaves through log
jams, backing quietly
into deep,
narrow
holes.
Meanwhile
we drive off the shy silvers
with loud clanking and clattering
of oars and loose gear as if
our driftboat were a tin pan
we bang on to scare off a moose.
Of course the salmon skedaddle.
We know he means well,
wants us to get our fish and not
just spend a long hot August
day on the Situk with seals
and otters and eagles and kingfishers,
but we are nearly skunked.
His words are all I pack
home from this float:
*fish the dead water hard.*

## *Tutka Bay Retreat*

A sucker for low tides, I walk the beach
instead of doing my homework. Abaft
a tombolo I spook a raft of ten
sea ducks that launch into two perfect
chevrons with military precision.
It's calm in here, but white sparks leap along
the opposing shore, wind burning the huff
of whale blows into smoke on the water.

I pick up a stranded half-size blue-green
star and toss it back. Why is it lovely?
It could be a grandfather to thousands.
We will make families of asterisks.

A fat sun-star scootches through the shallows,
lilac arm-tips flopping loose in the wavelets
as if broken, the stolid center mass
keeping its course, safety orange flashing
from the valleys between twenty ridges.
A sea nettle the size of my head pulses
just often enough to stay off the rocks.

There is something about those five-armed stars,
so symmetrical and yet not, balanced
and incomplete, like poetry, like life.

This record-dry summer stacked spawned-out pinks
at the mouths of skinny, inaccessible
streams, then last week's big rains washed them back out
to litter down-bay beaches with their bones.

## ACKNOWLEDGMENTS

Many colleagues at the University of Alaska Fairbanks have been supportive of my side gig as a poet over the years, offering me space to publish and opportunities to read in public (not to mention credit in my workload). Peggy Shumaker lured me out of the poetic closet decades ago at a poetry slam at the Pub, and has given me constructive criticism in the years since. The late great Burns Cooper offered to share the stage for my first public reading, and since then the Fairbanks Arts Association's monthly reading series has provided several additional opportunities to air out my poetry. In the last few years Emily Wall has offered excellent editorial suggestions and even more valuable encouragement; it's a fair bet this manuscript would never have seen print without her generosity. Sandy Kleven and Mike Burwell welcomed me with open arms, and Mike provided a keen editorial eye. Big thanks to David Mollet, from whom I bought my first piece of art after moving to Alaska, and who has kindly made his work available for this book. Thanks also to the hundreds of UAF students with whom I've been lucky enough to share the study of so many great poets—if you had not been willing to demonstrate through your excitement and hard work the enduring power of poetry, I would not have had the heart to keep on writing. Finally, I'm deeply grateful to the kith and kin who have allowed—and even at times encouraged—me to write out my very subjective version of some of our family history.

Versions of some of these poems have been previously published in the journals *Cirque, Ice-Floe, Big Tex(t), Arctica, Scintilla, Literary Laundry, Poecology, Bird's Thumb, and Shark Reef.*

## ABOUT THE AUTHOR

Eric Heyne has taught for thirty-five years in the English Department at the University of Alaska Fairbanks. He is the editor of two books—*Desert, Garden, Margin, Range: Literature on the American Frontier* and the University of Alaska Press edition of Jack London's *Burning Daylight*—and has published scholarship in *Modern Fiction Studies, Narrative, Critique, Extrapolation, The Northern Review, A Companion to the Literature and Culture of the American West*, and elsewhere. In addition to the journals mentioned in the Acknowledgments, he has published poems in *Alaska Quarterly Review, Platte Valley Review*, and elsewhere. He lives with his wife, Alexandra Fitts, on a south-facing slope above the Tanana Valley with a view of both distant mountains and close-up climate change.

## ABOUT CIRQUE PRESS

Cirque Press grew out of *Cirque*, a literary journal that publishes the works of writers and artists from the North Pacific Rim, a region that reaches north from Oregon to the Yukon Territory, south through Alaska to Hawaii, and west to the Russian Far East.

Cirque Press is a partnership of Sandra Kleven, publisher, and Michael Burwell, editor. Ten years ago, we recognized that works of talented writers in the region were going unpublished, and the Press was launched to bring those works to fruition. We publish fiction, non-fiction, and poetry, and we seek to produce art that provides a deeper understanding about the region and its cultures. The writing of our authors is significant, personal, and strong.

Sandra Kleven – Michael Burwell, publishers and editors
www.cirquejournal.com

## BOOKS FROM CIRQUE PRESS

*Apportioning the Light* by Karen Tschannen (2018)

*The Lure of Impermanence* by Carey Taylor (2018)

*Echolocation* by Kristin Berger (2018)

*Like Painted Kites & Collected Works* by Clifton Bates (2019)

*Athabaskan Fractal: Poems of the Far North* by Karla Linn Merrifield (2019)

*Holy Ghost Town* by Tim Sherry (2019)

*Drunk on Love: Twelve Stories to Savor Responsibly*
by Kerry Dean Feldman (2019)

*Wide Open Eyes: Surfacing from Vietnam* by Paul Kirk Haeder (2020)

*Silty Water People* by Vivian Faith Prescott (2020)

*Life Revised* by Leah Stenson (2020)

*Oasis Earth: Planet in Peril* by Rick Steiner (2020)

*The Way to Gaamaak Cove* by Doug Pope (2020)

*Loggers Don't Make Love* by Dave Rowan (2020)

*The Dream That Is Childhood* by Sandra Wassilie (2020)

*Seward Soundboard* by Sean Ulman (2020)

*The Fox Boy* by Gretchen Brinck (2021)

*Lily Is Leaving: Poems* by Leslie Ann Fried (2021)

*One Headlight* by Matt Caprioli (2021)

*November Reconsidered* by Marc Janssen (2021)

*Callie Comes of Age* by Dale Champlin (2021)

*Someday I'll Miss This Place Too* by Dan Branch (2021)

*Out There In The Out There* by Jerry McDonnell (2021)

*Fish the Dead Water Hard* by Eric Heyne (2021)

**CIRCLES**
Illustrated books from Cirque Press

*Baby Abe: A Lullaby for Lincoln* by Ann Chandonnet (2021)

*Miss Tami, Is Today Tomorrow?* by Tami Phelps (2021)

Made in the USA
Monee, IL
16 May 2022

96434208R00050